To my dear brother and partner in the Gospel.

Nothing happens by accident. He makes all things beautiful!

Daily Confessions for Victorious Living

Daily Confessions for Victorious Living
Copyright © 2013 by Dr. Emmanuel Favor
Published by First Fruits Publishing, LLC
Cover design by Honeyblue Imaging, LLC

Scripture taken from the New King James Version®.
Copyright © 1982 by Thomas Nelson, Inc. Used by permission. All rights reserved.
Printed in the United States of America
Signature Book Printing, www.sbpbooks.com

ISBN 13 978 0 9840618 3-9
ISBN 10 0 9840618-3-5

All rights reserved. No part of this publication may be reproduced or transmitted in any form or by any means, electronic or mechanical, including photocopy, recording, or any information storage retrieval system, without permission in writing from publisher. Requests for permission to make copies of any part of the work should be mailed to the following address: First Fruits Publishing, 9722 Groffs Mill Drive, P.O. Box 106, Owings Mills, MD. 21117

For more information about this work or this author contact First Fruits Publishing, LLC at
info@firstfruitspublishing.com

Table of Contents

Acknowledgements xi

Preface xiii

What Is A Confession? 1

Monday Confession 7

Tuesday Confession 13

Wednesday Confession 19

Thursday Confession 25

Friday Confession 29

Saturday Confession 33

Sunday Confession 39

Confessions for Financial Breakthrough 45

Confession for Self-Esteem 49

Confessions for Divine Healing 53

Confessions for Peace 57

Confessions for Your Church 61

Confessions for Tithes and Offerings 63

Confessions for Your Children 65

A Message From the Author 75

Dedication

This book is dedicated to my amazingly loving church family, for catching the vision and running with it. Greater things await us as we continue to persevere in prayer!

Daily Confessions for Victorious Living
Prayers of an Overcomer

Dr. Emmanuel Favor

Therefore I say to you, whatever things you ask when you pray, believe that you receive them, and you will have them.
(Mark 11:24, NKJV)

Acknowledgements

Anyone who has ever achieved anything of significance knows that a project such as this is never the result or the effort of a single individual, but the outcome and the contributions of many people who have helped both in tangible and intangible ways. This book is no exception.

As I think back over the years of my life and ministry, there are so many people who have helped me greatly along the way and without their assistance; I may never have gotten to the point of even writing this book. Acknowledging all of them and apportioning due credit for the roles they played and still do, would be humanly impossible to do, without leaving out someone crucial. Therefore, only in eternity will their true sacrifice and rewards be revealed. To each one of them, I say thank you.

In addition, I would like to acknowledge the following: my spiritual father, Dr. Creflo A. Dollar, for the impartation he has made into my life, Bishop I. V. Hilliard who first sowed the idea of this book in my heart, during one of his Strategies Conference, Minister Pam Phillips for initially editing the manuscript, Aaron and Deborah Dock who connected me with an incredibly supportive publisher, Kwanza Gipson and First Fruits Publishing for taking the manuscript and turning it into a book. There were many steps involved and many hands to do the work; to all of them, my sincere thanks and appreciation.

Most of all, I thank my Heavenly Father, who is truly my all in all! In Him everything began and in Him it is all contained.

Preface

Prayer is communing with God. In prayer we talk to God and share our heart with Him - our desires and apprehensions, as well as petitions and gratitude –knowing that He hears us and that He wants for us to know Him and His will for our lives. This type of fellowship is vital in developing a vibrant relationship with God.

From a biblical point of view, prayer is never supposed to be a spiritual chore or a means of obtaining righteousness. Instead, it should be seen as a spiritual exercise, most fruitful and benefitting when engaged in with the right motives. It is a means to intimate and personal fellowship with our Heavenly Father. Yet, for some people, praying can seem like a task that is both daunting and intimidating.

Anyone can pray to God, but not every prayer gets results. For prayer to be effective and make a difference, there are some key elements that must be applied. For instance, in order to pray effectively, it is important to first know the will of God, ask God in faith believing that you have received what you prayed for and begin thanking God even before there is any evidence or results of what you prayed for. So many people question whether prayer really works, when in fact the problem lies in how casual they approach prayer. Here is what the scripture says in 1 John 5:14-15:

"Now this is the confidence that we have in Him, that if we ask anything according to His will, He hears us. 15 And if we know that He hears us, whatever we ask, we know that we have the petitions that we have asked of Him."

When it comes to prayer, eloquence or the length of time one prays are not what makes prayer effective. You must simply speak to your Heavenly Father as you would your earthly parent. It is a conversation carried out in the context of a love relationship. Unfortunately, many people have never experienced a loving, supporting and respectful relationship with their earthly parent and therefore are unable to project the same feelings and confidence in their relationship with God.

As a pastor, it has been my privilege to teach and help people develop a prayer life and

Daily Confessions for Victorious Living

confidence in approaching God. I have seen first-hand the difference that prayer has made in my own life and countless others, who have decided to trust the Bible as the word of God and on that basis, engage in spiritual warfare through prayer. That is why I have written this book. It is intended to be a prayer training wheel for you, so that you can develop a strong and effective prayer life that is based on the word of God.

My desire and hope is that it will spur you to prayer, as well as help you know how to incorporate the will of God into your prayer. It contains a prayer format for each day of the week as well as many other situations that we face on a daily basis in life.

Spending time with the Father in prayer each day is surety for permanent, lasting change and positive results. When you pray, believe that you already have what you asked for and you will (Mark 11:24).

I encourage you to keep this book handy and use it as a guide in your daily life and see the manifestation of the promises of God's word.

What Is A Confession?

A confession is a declaration that we speak with our mouth. Most people associate the word confession with something negative, such as when someone confesses their sins or admits guilt. However, confession does not only have to do with sin. It can be an admission of sin as well as a profession of faith. Whatever we speak out is a confession.

Confession means to say the same thing. In this case, we are saying the same thing as God says over us. When God's word says that we are blessed, then we are to echo what God says, and say, "I am blessed," or "healed", or "prosperous."

Our confession is a powerful force, because the Bible tells us in Mark 11:20-23, that we will have whatever we say.

Why Is Our Confession Important?

The scripture states in Proverbs 18: 21 that, "Life and death are in the power of the tongue". The tongue is a powerful tool that determines both death and life. Since we desire life, it only makes sense that we should use what we have been given to create what we desire. What do you desire? It's in your mouth.

The word of God spoken in faith by a believer carries creative abilities. Words become self-fulfilling prophecies. That is why our confession is important. However, we must be diligent to ensure that our words and confessions are in line with the Word of God.

God's word created the universe that we see and experience around us. God spoke everything into existence. Since we were made in the image of God and in His likeness, we too can create our realities through the words we speak.

Prayer of Confession

Prayer is when we speak to the Father, from our hearts. It's an intimate and personal time with our Father where we can tell Him our true desires and have the confidence of knowing that He hears us.

The prayer of confession is called prophecy. Prophecy is when we speak the mind of God. The word of God is the mind of God. When we confess the word of God, we are prophesying.

Biblical Examples of the Prayer of Confession

The case of Jesus and the fig tree in Mark 11:12 –14, 20 – 24 is an example of confession. Jesus spoke the word, but there was no immediate or visible effect on the tree. It took time before the evidence could be seen. What Jesus spoke out of His mouth came to pass.

Another example of the prayer of confession is the case of Ezekiel and the dry bones in Ezekiel 37:1 – 14. Ezekiel only had to speak God's will over the dry bones. The words that Ezekiel spoke brought life back to the dry bones.

Life does not have to depend on what we see at the moment. There is power at work beyond what the eyes can see. We can activate that power and set it to work for us, by our confession.

Dr. Emmanuel Favor

Daily Confessions for Victorious Living

*Now this is the confidence that we have in Him, that if we ask anything according to His will, He hears us. And if we know that He hears us, whatever we ask, we know that we have the petitions that we have asked of Him.
(1 John 5:14-15, NKJV)*

Dr. Emmanuel Favor

Monday Confession

"...He will be very gracious to you at the sound of your cry; when He shall hear it, He will answer you." (Isaiah 30:19, NKJV)

Father in the name of Jesus, I thank You for another day and the beginning of another work week. I thank You because You prepared this day for me, long before the foundation of the earth. I thank You that I was put here by You to accomplish a purpose prepared especially for me. I thank You that this day is pregnant with blessings, potential and opportunities.

Father, I ask You to give me the grace needed for today's assignment. I thank You that You have heard me; therefore, I believe that I receive the empowerment to make the best of this day. I will be productive, resourceful and fruitful in all that I set my hands to do.

I acknowledge You in all my plans and goals for this week. I thank You that You have given me Your Spirit to lead and guide me always. Therefore, I rely on the Holy Spirit to help me prioritize my day, to help me discern the value of each task, and to assist me in implementing the best plans. I yield and defer to Your leading. I thank You that I am smart, I am witty and I can do all things through Christ that gives me strength.

Today, I pray for my immediate family, ~~my spouse, (name)~~ and my children (names). I cover them with the favor of God. I call God's protection over them. I build a spiritual pavilion over their lives. The sun shall not smite them by day nor the moon by night. I thank You that You have given Your angels charge over them. Angels will guide them in all their ways, and bear them up, and they shall not dash their feet against any stone. Goodness and mercy will be their portion because they are the seed of the righteous.

I pray that no evil arrow will find them. No intentions of the enemy will be fulfilled on them. I pray for my children as they go to school this week and as they interact with other children that no negative influence will sway them. They will shine as light in darkness and darkness cannot overcome or overtake them.

I declare that my offspring will never fall victim to abuse of any kind; no molestation, no prejudice, and no neglect. I cover them from the influence of the godless. My children will never experiment with drugs, alcohol or sex. All my children will remain virgins until their wedding. I thank You that their minds are infused with the truth. I thank You that my children have been saved at a young age and that they will continue in the truth for the rest of their lives.

Father, I plead the blood of Jesus over my children's future. I declare that they will not make the same mistakes that I have made. They will not stumble over the things that I have stumbled over. I thank You that my children have the benefit of godly parents and role models. I declare that the curse of my ancestors shall be foreign to my children. I declare that they are the blessed of the Lord. I thank You that their names are self-fulfilling prophecies; as their names are, so also are their destinies: a delightful fragrance, a victorious champion and a wealth gatherer.

The Word declares that death and life are in the power of the tongue, therefore with my tongue I declare life over my children. With long life You will satisfy them. I give You praise for their lives in Jesus' name.

Father, I thank You that my spouse is a gift from You. I thank You that she/he is in my life. I appreciate him/her and honor him/her. I commit myself to him/her. I covenant that I will remain faithful to him/her for the rest of my life. I thank You that she/he pleases me. I am delighted in her/him, and I delight her/him. I call her/him what You call her/him:

For the WIFE: a virtuous woman, a fruitful branch, the daughter of Zion. She shall never be defiled. She is most honorable among women.

For the HUSBAND: I call him a mighty man of God: a priest, a prophet, a king, a warrior, the head and not the tail, a great nation.

I thank You that my wife/husband knows who she/he is in Christ. He/She knows his/her value, and he/she is confident in himself/herself and in his/her calling. I thank You for he/she is an embodiment of gifts and talents. I thank You for the value that he/she brings into my life and our children's lives. I thank You that our marriage is a model in the Kingdom; through our lifestyle, many will choose the path of righteousness. I confess that we have a beyond average marriage. We have a supernatural marriage.

Thank You Father for giving me the desires of my heart, through my wife/husband. I thank You that she/he is everything I would ever want in a wife/husband. She/He is everything a child would ever want in a mother/father.

Father, once again I praise You with all my heart, for hearing my prayers and granting my petitions. I present these petitions in the name of Your begotten Son Jesus Christ. And I thank You that because I have done so, I now receive them, in Jesus' name. Amen!

Dr. Emmanuel Favor

Tuesday Confession

"Praying always with all prayer and supplication in the Spirit, being watchful to this end with all perseverance and supplication for all the saints…" (Ephesians 6:18, NKJV)

Father, I thank You today that I am alive and well, living in Your grace. I thank You for victories that You won for me in the past. I thank You because You are ever present to help me when I am in trouble. You are the lifter of my head.

I thank You that You have placed me in a loving and caring church family. I thank You for my brothers and sisters, in the Lord. I thank You for every member, every worker and every leader in our church. Thank You that You have set my church as a house upon the hill that cannot be hidden. Thank You that You have positioned us in a place of influence and authority in the land. Just as Your word says, the mountain of the house of the

Lord shall be exalted above all the hills, and the people shall flow to it.

I declare that people will continually flow to God's house. They are coming from every direction, from every walk of life, from every age group and from every social level. I call forth multitudes to come from the North, the South, the East and the West. And as they come, they are discovering God's purpose for their lives; they are connecting with the living Word.

Father, I pray for my brothers and sisters in Christ, whatever challenges they are facing this week; I stand in the gap for them to experience grace to see them through. I pray for those who are experiencing loneliness that they will find authentic connection in the family of God and build meaningful friendships. I pray for the sick and confess their total healing and recovery. I call every sick in the house of God healed in Jesus' name. I call every diseased well. I call every bound liberated, every broken mended; I command the healing power of God upon the sick, from their heads to their toes.

I pray for those who are new in our church family; I receive them warmly and with love. I pray for them to be rooted and grounded in their set places. I pray that their hearts will not be discouraged by things they may not yet understand. I pray that their hearts will not be abused by the negative opinions of people. I pray for steadfastness and faithfulness in their hearts. I thank You that just as You have called them to our family, You will also keep and sustain them.

Father, thank You that You have planted them where they will be fruitful; they will flourish and be productive.

I pray and lift up all on-going projects in our church before You; in faith I ask and trust You for supernatural supply of funds and other resources so that each project will be successfully completed. I thank You that no assignment in the house will ever stall for lack of funds. I command money to flow into the ministry.

I come against every plan of the enemy to hinder, slow down, or abort the work in God's house. I declare that such attempts shall be like the efforts of Sanballat and Tobiah, who tried to hinder Nehemiah, but were woefully unsuccessful. I command every satanic opposition against Your kingdom endeavors to cease. I declare victory in the name of Jesus.

I pray for our television ministry. I thank You for the opportunity to take the Gospel to the multitudes through the media. I pray that this week, more people will be reached for Christ. I pray for those who will watch our broadcast this week that they will hear something, experience something and see something that will make an impact in their destiny. I thank You for the word seed that will be sown, watered or harvested. I thank You for results manifesting in different stages in the lives of people. I thank You for grace upon my pastor to connect with the masses so that they are receptive to the Gospel.

I pray for every person who is serving in ministry in our church. I thank You for their dedication and commitment. I thank You that the dedication they sow into the ministry will come back to them in abounding measure. I thank You for the promise of Your word that whoever shall leave father, mother, brother, sister or house for Christ sake and the Kingdom sake, will receive in this life, a hundred fold. I pray for that hundred fold increase to be upon every worker in the Kingdom.

Daily Confessions for Victorious Living

I pray for all the coordinators in my church that they will serve and lead with integrity. I thank You Father that they are catching the spirit of excellence and they are in unity. I come against every spirit of division among our leaders. I declare the peace of God over them and their families. I bless them as leaders. I thank You that they are growing in the word, in leadership and in discernment.

Father, I bless Your holy name because You always hear me when I pray. Therefore, I believe that I receive my petitions today, in Jesus' name. Amen!

Dr. Emmanuel Favor

Wednesday Confession

"Be anxious for nothing, but in everything by prayer and supplication, with thanksgiving, let your request be made known to God." (Philippians 4:6, NKJV)

Dear Father in Heaven, I worship You this day as my Lord and my God. You sit on a throne that is higher than all others. Your glory is greater than all. You are the greatest and Your name is most holy and powerful in all the earth. I worship You for who You are. I magnify You and bow before You, in humble adoration.

I thank You that You have showered me with goodness, kindness and mercy. I praise Your name for all that Your hand has provided for me. I thank You for Your promises to me.

The word exhorts that first of all supplications, prayers, intercessions, and giving of thanks be made for all men, for kings and all who are in authority, that we may lead a quiet and peaceable life in all godliness and reverence. So Father, this day I come before Your holy presence to offer my prayer, supplication and intercession for my city, my state and my nation.

It is not by accident or by mere coincidence that I am living in this city at this time. I believe that You have placed me in this city for a purpose and for a time such as this. By Your divine design You have planted me where You intend for me to flourish. So I declare that this is my set place. It is my place of assignment, my mission field and my set place of blessing and increase.

Moreover, I thank You that I am salt and light. Therefore, my presence in this land is retardant to the forces of darkness. I come against the forces of darkness in this city. I lift up the banner of the blood of Jesus over my city. I declare that this city belongs to Christ. By His blood, He paid the price for the redemption of the whole world, which includes my city. So in the name of Jesus _____ (name Your city) belongs to Jesus. I sprinkle the blood around the limits of this city. I put a blood mark boundary against the spirit of darkness. I declare that Satan and his demons have no place in my city, in the name of Jesus.

Daily Confessions for Victorious Living

I declare my city free from every form of demonic oppression; I call this city drug free, prostitution free, violence free, and murder free in the name of Jesus. I pray that the people will become passionate about exposing perpetrators, and willing to cooperate with law enforcement agencies. I pray for our law enforcement agents to be men and women of integrity and honesty, free from corruption.

Father, I pray for the leaders of my state that Your hand is continually upon them to guide and lead them, even though they themselves may not confess or acknowledge You as Lord. Righteousness exalts a nation, but sin is a reproach to any people; therefore we take the side of righteousness and pray that righteousness will prevail in the corridors of power and government, in the name of Jesus.

I pray for all the city mayors in this United States of America. I pray for every governor of every state, every law maker, every councilman and woman, every member of the House of Representatives, every senator and for all those who are in authority. I pray that in one way or the other, Your spirit will influence them, direct them, guide them and motivate them in their decision making. I pray that You expose and remove every hidden agenda. Expose and remove individuals who do not have the best interest of the people they lead at heart. Expose and remove corrupt politicians, policemen and judges. I pray for the judiciary arm of government. I pray that they will be just, fair and truthful. I pray that the men and women to whom have been entrusted the responsibility of upholding the law and dispensing justice, will do so with fairness and equity. I pray that You rule in the hearts and minds of judges.

Father, I thank You for America. I thank You that I live in this great nation. I bless America. I pray for the peace of America and the peace of Israel. I bless Israel, its people, its leaders and its national endeavours.

I pray that You forgive America for turning her back on the values that made her great. I confess the sins of my people, my household and even my own sins that have made America weak. I pray that we as a nation will turn wholeheartedly to God and honor the values upon which this nation was founded.

I claim peace for America. I declare every terrorist plot to destroy innocent lives null and void. Their plots shall be uncovered and no weapon formed against us shall prosper. I pray no attack shall ever succeed within the borders of this nation.

Father, I thank You for hearing my prayers. I thank You that because of the prayers of the righteous, Your blessings will continue to cover our communities, our cities and this nation. It is in Jesus' name that I pray, Amen!

Dr. Emmanuel Favor

Thursday Confession

"Now hope does not disappoint, because the love of God has been poured out in our hearts by the Holy Spirit who was given to us." (Romans 5:5, NKJV)

Father, I thank You for this is the day that You have made; therefore I will rejoice and I will be glad in it. My soul shall make its boast in You, for You alone are the lifter of my head. You are my shield and my defense. You are my stronghold; You make my mountain stand strong and the lines have fallen to me in pleasant places.

I say like David, I will bless the LORD who has given me counsel. I have set the LORD always before me; because He is at my right hand, I shall not be moved. Therefore, my heart is glad, and my glory rejoices; my flesh also will rest in hope.

Today, I intentionally renew my dedication to You. I choose to abide in You and allow Your word to abide in me. I have found Your love to be better than life itself. Nothing compares to knowing You, loving You, and living in Your grace.

Father, I am grateful that I know You. Thank You that my eyes have been opened to the truth. Thank You that I have experienced the light; thank You that I can come into Your presence. Thank You that I am saved, by Your grace.

I offer to You this day, myself as a living sacrifice, holy and acceptable to You. I offer You all that I am and all that I have. Lord, I belong to You. Do with me as You will. Use me for Your glory. Use me to be a blessing; to fulfil Your desire. Let my life give You pleasure, so I may fulfil the purpose for which I was created.

As the deer pants for water, so my soul longs for You. I long to please You, to live for You and to know You more. I thank You that You are satisfying my deepest longings. Your spirit is pouring upon me like water. Your word is taking root in my heart; therefore, sin is far from me. I hide Your word in my heart. It is the light that guides me and directs my steps.

I thank You Lord that Your love for me has no boundaries. I thank You that I am kept by Your unfailing power. I thank You that I am preserved by Your unending grace. I thank You that I am surrounded by Your favor. I am directed by Your kindness.

In Your presence there is fullness of joy and at Your right hand there are pleasures for evermore. One day in Your courts is better than a thousand days elsewhere. I commit myself to seeking Your face and dwelling in Your presence.

I thank You, that he who dwells in the secret place of the most high shall abide under the shadow of the Almighty. I am continually covered by the shadow of Your wings. This day I break free from every form of carnality. I reject the tendencies of the flesh in the name of the Lord. I reject every tendency to be impatient and in haste. I wait patiently upon the Lord, for in His time, He makes all things beautiful.

It is written, *"call upon me and I will answer You and show You great and mighty things that You know not of."* I call upon the Lord this day, and I thank You that You answer me and You cause me to see Your greatness.

They that trust in the Lord shall be like Mount Zion, which cannot be moved. I confess that I am like a mountain. I can never be moved. I cannot be moved in my conviction; I cannot be moved in my confession of faith and I cannot be moved in my commitment to righteousness.

I dedicate myself to You this day. I choose obedience over sacrifice. I make a conscious commitment to walk in obedience to You in every area of my life. I thank You that You have commanded blessings to pursue and overtake me, in my going out and in my coming in.

This is my day of renewal; thank You, for You make all things new. My faith is renewed, my mind is renewed, my dedication is renewed, my love is renewed and Your spirit is renewed in me today. I give You praise and glory. In Jesus' precious name, Amen!

Friday Confession

"He shall call upon Me, and I will answer him; I will be with him in trouble; I will deliver him and honor him. With long life I will satisfy him, and show him my salvation." (Psalm 91:15-16, NKJV)

Father, I thank You for Your plans for my life which cover every area of my life – my spirit, soul and body. I thank You that You are a good God and You take care of all my needs. You supply all my needs according to Your riches in glory by Christ Jesus.

I thank You this day. I pray that You have placed upon me the anointing of distinction that sets me above and never beneath; so that I am the head and not the tail. I thank You for this is Your ultimate desire for me.

I pray for the anointing of prosperity that is upon me, to produce accordingly. I release the grace to be fruitful and prosperous in every area of my life. I employ the favor of God in all my endeavours, for You Lord will bless the righteous; with favor You will surround him as with a shield. Therefore, I am surrounded by favor.

I activate the grace for steady increase in my life. I shall continue to increase and be financially blessed to the point that I will become a lender and not a borrower. I take authority over every spirit of waste. I cast it far from me. No good thing shall be wasted in my life.

Father, I ask that You make me a giver, for You love a cheerful giver. I pray for the sensitivity to see needs in the kingdom and the grace to willingly meet the needs in the lives of others.

I pray for divine health so that my body will always be in good condition to serve You faithfully. I command my body to be healed of any ailment in the name of Jesus. I pray for those who need healing and good health.

By faith, I receive their healing in the mighty name of Jesus Christ. I command sickness, diseases and afflictions to be far from them. I thank You, that by the stripes of Jesus they are healed. I thank You for the manifestation of their healing.

6. HILLARY CLINTON
7. TIM KAINE

Daily Confessions for Victorious Living

5. DR EMMANUEL FAVOR

I thank You for the authority to stand in the gap for the needs of others. Right now I bring the following individuals before You and intercede for every need in their lives to be met, according to Your mighty power and gracious hand:

1. ~~JANET~~
2. ~~JAMES JR~~
3. ~~EDMUND~~
4. ~~JAMES SR~~
5. ~~KRISTOPHER~~
6. RICHARD CLAIBORNE

I thank You that every burden is lifted from them and every yoke is destroyed in the name of Jesus. I call the peace of God over them. I pray the favor of God to surround them. I speak increase, blessing, abundance and soundness in Jesus' name, Amen.

7. DANIELL ROACHE
8. ~~EUGENE ROACHE~~
9. ~~EUGENE ROACHE III~~
10. ~~DANIEL CLAIBORNE~~
11. ~~CHEVON CLAIBORNE~~
12. NAILAH CLAIBORNE
13. ~~JENNIFER CLAIBORNE~~
14. NASIR CLAIBORNE
15. ~~ELIJAH GRANT~~
16. ~~ZACHARY~~
17. ALEXANDRIA WILLIS
18. ~~ALEXANDRIA HARRIS~~
19. ~~JAI-DEN HARRIS~~ WILLIS
20. APRIL CASON
21. ~~ELLISON CASON~~
22. ~~JOSHUA CASON~~
23. AUSTIN CASON
25. CHRISTINA
26. ~~BARBARA HARRIS~~
27. LAUREN SEEBERGEN
28. STEPHANIE ACOSTA
29. JOSE ACOSTA

OVER

Dr. Emmanuel Favor

30. JOSE ACOSTA JR
31. LEAH ACOSTA
32. ~~ALLISON~~
33. ~~DAVID~~
34. ~~DAVE SEEBERGER~~
35. MELODY ACOSTA, ~~MELINIE~~ MELANIE
36. JEFFERSON O'NEAL
~~37. D. ANDRE~~
37. D'ANDERA HIERS SR
38. RAY RICE
39. ~~BILL CROSBY~~
40. ~~CALVIN CHOLATON~~
41. ~~JIMMIE POWE~~ SR
42. ~~JIMMIE POWE (BABY)~~ JR
43. JACQUELINE JONES
44. NATHAN H. SEEBERGER

Saturday Confession

"My son, give attention to my words; incline your ear to my sayings. Do not let them depart from your eyes; keep them in the midst of your heart; for they are life to those who find them, and health to all their flesh." (Proverbs 4:20-22, NKJV)

Heavenly Father, Creator of heaven and earth, thank You that Your ears are always open to hear me. Thank You that Your eyes are always upon me. You are ever mindful of Your covenant with me. I am so blessed to know that You know me by name and You have plans for me.

I worship You, because You are my God and my Lord. You are the beauty of my life. You are the all sufficient One. To You be all glory, because You give meaning to my life. Thank You that You found me and brought me into Your ligth. Thank You that You have caused me to know You. Thank You that You have opened my eyes to Your truth and made my heart receptive of Your word.

My lips praise You and my heart rejoices in Your salvation. You are the anchor of my soul, the hope of my future and the confidence of my faith. In You I live and move and have my being. In You, I will forever boast, because You are my strong tower.

Today, as I begin my day, I do so knowing that You are with me. Your presence is ever with me. You have promised never to leave me, nor forsake me. Your rod and Your staff, they comfort me. You prepare a table before me, in the presence of my enemies and Your banner over me is love.

I love You my Heavenly Father, with all my heart. I trust Your word and I find my hope and comfort in Your promises. I put sin and unrighteousness far away from me. I turn from everything that is not pleasing to You. I purge my heart of every sin and every weight.

Father, I ask of You this day, give me grace to forgive and release every person who has hurt or wronged me. I release every offense that I may have in my heart against them. I cover my heart with the blood of Jesus and I refuse to harbor offense and bitterness. I forgive people who have hurt me; I forgive the people who have spoken ill about me. I

Daily Confessions for Victorious Living

forgive those who may have acted negatively towards me. I confess that I love them, in spite of how they have treated me. I pray for their well-being and I ask You to forgive them and to bless them abundantly. I pray for the following individuals that You grant me the grace to love them unconditionally:

1. JANET CLAIBORNE
2. JAMES HARRIS JR
3. EDMUND HARRIS
4. KRISTOPHER HARRIS
5. JEFFERSON ONEAL
6. D'ANDRE (ANDERA) / RICHARD CLAIBORNE / HIER SR

I pray for people who have authority over me. I pray that You give them wisdom in their position for leadership, so they may do what is right and pleasing to You. I pray for those who are under my leadership. Make me the type of leader that they want to willingly follow. Help me to be sensitive to their needs. Make me attentive to Your directives and help me to be able to discern what is from You and what is not.

I pray for my extended family members. I stand upon Your promise that me and my house shall serve the Lord. Therefore, I claim salvation for all my extended family members. I call them by name:

1. JEFFERSON ONEAL
2. DR EMMUNUEL FAVOR
3. ~~D'ANDRE~~ D'ANDERA HIERS SR
4. TICC MEMBERS
5. ALL MY FAMILY MEMBERS

    I pray that every one of them will make it to heaven. I pray for their eyes to be opened to the truth of their need for Jesus Christ as Savior. I pray that You grant me opportunities to share Christ with them. I pray that You raise others who will also witness about the Lord to all my family members. I pray that their hearts will be receptive to the word.

    Father, I thank You in advance for the salvation testimony of every single one of them. I praise You for Your grace will reach deep and far to find each and every single one of my family members.

    Thank You Father for Your love and mercies over me and my household. Lead me this day and show me the path that You have laid out for me. I thank You that I will be sensitive to Your voice throughout this day.

I declare that I will be a blessing to someone today. I thank You that I will be an answer to someone's need today. In the same way, I receive my destiny helpers today. You will bring me into the company of those You have ordained to impact my life.

To You be the praise and glory for all these things, in Jesus' name. Amen!

Sunday Confession

"Therefore He is also able to save to the uttermost those who come to God through Him, since He always lives to make intercession for them." (Hebrews 7:25, NKJV)

Father, in the name of Jesus I thank You today that I am in the land of the living. The word says that the living must praise You; therefore, I praise You this day with everything that is in me.

I thank You because this is the day that You have made. I rejoice in this day and I make my boast in You and You alone. I thank You for the privilege of being part of the family of God. I thank You that today I will participate in corporate worship together with my church family. I am both grateful and excited about the opportunity to be numbered among the saints of God; God's best and God's dearest.

I prepare my heart right now so that I will hear Your voice in the worship celebration. I put away every distraction and I make You the focus of my attention. Today, when I am taught the word of God, my mind will be alert, my spirit will be receptive and I will receive revelation knowledge freely out of Your word.

I pray for my Pastor. I thank You that You have prepared him/her as a vessel to speak Your word to me. I thank You that You will make his/her tongue like the pen of a ready writer, inscribing eternal truths upon the hearts of Your people. I thank You that my pastor is anointed with a word for today. I declare that there will be a mighty presence of God in the service today. Every burden will be totally lifted and no yoke will remain undestroyed over the lives of Your people.

Father, I cover my Pastor and his/her family with the goodness of the Lord. I pray that no evil will come upon them. I pray for my pastor and his/her family, that the love of Christ be seen in them. I come against every satanic plot against them. I call heaven to be opened over them. I pray that You reveal, expose and remove anyone around them who is an agent of the enemy, posing as a friend. I pray that You reveal, expose and remove anyone in leadership or staff of the church, who does not have the best interest of my pastor, his vision or of the church, at heart. I thank You for surrounding my pastor with faithful, creative and loyal staff.

I come against every form of satanic and demonic interference in the worship celebration today. I resist every temptation to be carried away and distracted by what other people are doing or not doing. I resist the temptation of rejecting the truth simply because it does not line up with what I think or already know. I open my heart and mind to receive fresh revelation and understanding of the Word that is able to give me an inheritance among the sanctified.

I pray for every ministry that will be operating in the service today that they do so with excellence and holy passion. I pray for the praise and worship team. I pray for every usher to be sensitive to the Spirit. I pray for every greeter to communicate the love of Christ to those they come in contact with. I pray for the service coordinators that utterance be given them to speak a word in service that will lift up the worshippers. I pray for the media team, the sound team and all those who work behind the scenes to make the service run in excellence. Thank You Father, for You have set them apart to operate under the anointing of the Spirit today.

I pray for the guests that will be visiting our church today; they will experience the presence of God. In the name of Jesus, I believe with my pastor for a harvest of souls and finances into the kingdom of God. I call souls to be saved today. I call people to come. I call money to come. I call the right workers to come. I call everything to fall into their place in Jesus' name.

I thank You Father that You have made all things beautiful and everything is in place for a life changing celebration today. Thank You for healings that will take place. Thank You for deliverances. Thank You for transformation. And thank You that You will touch each person at their point of need.

I thank You in advance for all that You will do, because I pray in the matchless, most powerful name of Jesus Christ. Amen!

Confessions for Victorious Living Over Every Situation

*Then He spoke a parable to them that men always ought to pray and not lose heart
(Luke 18:1, NKJV)*

Dr. Emmanuel Favor

Confessions for Financial Breakthrough

"The blessing of the Lord makes one rich, and He adds no sorrow with it." (Proverbs 10:22, NKJV)

Dear Father, I thank You right now that I am in a covenant relationship with You. I thank You that Your covenant with me can never be broken. I thank You that You have covenanted to meet all my needs according to Your glorious riches. When I delight myself in You. And because I have made You my delight, I am positioned to receive every desire of my heart. You have made me the head and not the tail. My security is not in my bank statement, but in Your covenant with me.

I thank You that financial increase and material abundance is Your will for me. It is Your will for me to be in health and to prosper in all things. I agree with Your word and I call for a new season of financial breakthrough to begin in my life.

I thank You, for You have anointed my eyes to identify the hidden riches of this world; You have opened my eyes to see the secret to wealth. I command every hidden treasure of abundance to be exposed to me. I thank You that the riches of the ungodly are being turned into my hands.

I command increase and favor on all that belongs to me. I command my investments to grow exceedingly. I command my seed to produce according to covenant terms: good measure, pressed down, shaken together and running over.

Father, I pray for accelerated breakthrough, so the plowman overtakes the reaper. I declare right now that I shall reap an exponential harvest from every seed I have sown. I prophesy Psalm 112 verse 3 upon me: wealth and riches are in my house, and my righteousness will endure forever.

I take authority over the devourer that seeks to destroy my effort and righteous labor. I declare the plans of the enemy against my finances, null and void. By faith, I receive the blessing reserved for the righteous. I declare that I am like a tree planted by the rivers of water; I bring forth fruit in due season. And whatever my hands touch must prosper.

I reject lack and financial hardship. My God is the God of more than enough. Therefore, I will never lack any good thing in my life. I thank You Father that You do not withhold anything good from me.

I thank You that I shall want for nothing. I thank You that I am a giver. I am a generous seed sower in the Kingdom. I thank You that I have received the grace to sow without considering the adverse circumstances. I thank You for putting Your blessing on the seed and upon me, in Jesus' name. Amen!

Confession for Self-Esteem

"Being confident of this very thing, that He who has begun a good work in you will complete it until the day of Jesus Christ." (Philippians 1:6, NKJV)

Father I thank You that You have set me free from the bondages of insecurity and low self-esteem. I thank You that I am who You say that I am. I accept Your word as final verdict over my life: my past, my present and my future.

I acknowledge that my true identity and potential is not limited to my ability or credentials. But my true potential lies in You.

I thank You that You have opened my eyes to see beyond the flesh. According to Your word in 2 Corinthians 5:16, which says, "Therefore from now on we regard no one according to the flesh," even so, I do not regard myself according to the definitions of my flesh. Instead, I see myself through the mirror of Your word. I am truly special, valuable, loveable and teachable. I walk in dignity at all times.

I thank You that You know me more intimately than anyone else. You know me even better than I know myself. And Your opinion of me is positive. I thank You that I am not condemned to the mistakes of my past. I thank You that I am not what those who know me say that I am. Even though I may have failed in my relationship with them, I thank You that there is more virtue in me than what they see in me. I confess that the good in me is manifesting to God's glory.

Father, today I ask of You, to help me continually see myself from Your point of view. By faith, I ask and believe that I receive the wisdom to conduct my affairs according to Your will, so that my future becomes even brighter each day. I ask of You to silence the naysayers for my sake, by turning around every negative expectation concerning me. I repent and reject all the lies I have believed about me. I take authority over the things and voices that try to belittle me. I reject every form of self-condemnation, in the name of Jesus.

I break every hold of evil pronouncements made over my life. I break the power and hold of self-pity over me. I break the power of every type of emotional bondage that causes me to act without prudence. I thank You for the ability to face the future without any fear or anxiety. I thank You, for my expectations shall not be cut off. I thank You for turning the negative conclusions that people have made concerning me, into positive outcomes. I confess that I have dominion over every challenge I face.

Father, I give You praise for always causing me to have victory in the Lord Jesus. Thank You for choosing to make my body the temple of Your Holy Spirit. Thank You for paying such a high price for the redemption of my soul.

Holy Spirit, I invite You to transform and renew my mind; help me to accept the personality that You have given me. I come against every form of self-rejection and destruction in the name of Jesus. I find my true self-worth in Christ, at all times.

In the name of Jesus, I come against every tendency of the enemy to steal my joy, or godly self-confidence. I receive the grace to stay motivated at all times. Holy Spirit, I thank You that You have anointed me to be an over-comer and a finisher. I thank You that I am free from self-centeredness and from every form of self-abuse.

I thank You Jesus for making me complete in You, despite who I used to be. You are my redeemer and deliverer. I thank You that in You, I am whole and fit for life.

I thank You Father, for it is in You that I now move and live and have my being. I thank You for declaring me to be righteous. I rejoice that Your word says You are mindful of me. I thank You for choosing and using me for Your glory, despite my shortcomings.

I confess that each day I am growing to be more like Christ, in Jesus' name! Amen

Confessions for Divine Healing

"Surely He has borne our griefs and carried our sorrows…but He was wounded for our transgressions, He was bruised for our iniquities; the chastisement for our peace was upon Him, and by His stripes we are healed." (Isaiah 53:4-5, NKJV)

Father in the name of Jesus, I receive by faith the promise of healing contained in scripture. Surely Christ has borne my grief and carried my sorrows.

I thank You that Jesus was wounded for my transgressions, He was bruised for my iniquities; the chastisement for my peace was upon Him, and by His stripes I am forever healed.

I bind every sickness and disease that the enemy wants to put upon me. I declare that nothing will stop my destiny, nor hinder me from achieving my vision. I plead the blood of Jesus against every form of torment, whether physical, spiritual or emotional. I overturn every satanic oppression or suppression.

I declare boldly that Christ himself carried all my sorrows, all my pain and all my afflictions; therefore, I do not need to carry them. I thank You for You are the Lord my Healer. I thank You for revealing Yourself to me as Jehovah Rapha, the Lord who heals me.

I praise You Father for the opportunity to be alive and healthy, with nothing missing and nothing broken in my life. I declare that I am healed from my head to my toes. I bind every form of sickness from my body. I declare that every organ in me is functioning according to divine plan and purpose. Every nerve, every ligament, every tissue, every bone, and every cell is healthy, normal and functional.

I cancel every curse over my life. I break the hold of genetic diseases that run in my family, from binding me. I declare that it shall not be upon me. The disease of my ancestors has no power over me or my seed after me.

I seal every loophole that the enemy might have found to afflict me, such as disobedience, unforgiveness, lust or any other sin. I release every offense. I repent from hidden sins. I deny Satan the opportunity to torment and frustrate me. Affliction shall be far from me forever. And oppression shall be foreign to me.

I thank You for the times You have healed me in the past and I praise You that You continue to heal me now. I thank You that I am enjoying divine health and healing all the days of my life. I lift up the name of Jesus over sickness and disease.

I confess that through me, Your healing power is flowing to the people around me. I pray for the members of my household to receive the healing of the Lord. I thank You that the miracle of my healing will be a sign and wonder to the unsaved, leading them to Jesus.

I reject the lie of the devil that sickness glorifies God. I turn over every form of ailment which the doctors have said cannot be healed to You and I receive Your healing.

Thank You Lord for loving me so much and for taking care of every part of me. I praise You in Jesus' name!

Dr. Emmanuel Favor

Confessions for Peace

"...and the peace of God, which surpasses all understanding, will guard your hearts and minds through Christ Jesus." (Philippians 4:7, NKJV)

Heavenly Father, I thank You that Jesus Christ is my Prince of peace. I thank You that in Him I am complete, safe and secure. I thank You for angelic protection over me; You have released Your angels to guard and keep watch over me always.

I pray now in the name of Jesus, that You deliver me from unnecessary suspicion and fear. I receive the peace that breaks the power of fear. I claim my victory over every spirit of fear. I declare victory over the fear of death, the fear of failure, the fear of heights, the fear of flight, the fear of people, the fear of walking by faith and every other type of fear.

Father, I thank You that You always hear me when I pray. Even now, I know that You hear me; and because You hear me, I know that my petition is granted. I believe that I receive the peace of God. You are keeping me in perfect peace, because my mind is stayed on You.

I have the peace that the world cannot provide; I have unspeakable peace, which comes only from You. I rejoice right now because I am filled with the peace and joy of the Holy Spirit that flows in God's Kingdom.

I proclaim that You are my peace over troubled waters. You are my peace when I face challenges. You are my peace when the enemy rises like a boisterous tide against me. You are the lifter of my head. You have given Your angels charge over me; in their hands they bear me up, lest I dash my foot against a stone.

I thank You that You have enlarged the path from under me, so that my foot does not slip. I walk in the highway of life. I enjoy preferential treatment everywhere I go. I find favor before God and before men, because I am a child of the King.

I thank You that You keep Your promises towards me. You preserve my going out and my coming in. You give me peace in the land where in I

Daily Confessions for Victorious Living

dwell. Like Solomon, I am surrounded with the peace of God and nothing shall make me afraid. My ears shall continually hear good tidings. Affliction shall remain far from me.

Lord I worship You, because You have anointed me and filled my life with praise. My mouth shall continue to declare Your goodness. By faith, I release the peace of God in all my relationships. I release the peace of God in all my decisions. The peace of God is my umpire. It shall guide all my steps and decisions.

I thank You Lord for peace and the joy of answered prayers. I pray for this same peace to reign in the lives of my friends and family. I stand against any display of evil and torment in their lives. I speak the peace of God to every battle raging in their hearts.

Holy Spirit thank You that You garrison my heart with the peace that passes all understanding. Even in crisis, I will perceive in my spirit, the peace of God multiplying and leading me.

I thank You Father that I am fortified in Your presence. I praise You with all my heart. I thank You that I am free indeed, because Your Son has made me free. In Jesus' precious name, Amen!

Confessions for Your Church

"Be kindly affectionate to one another with brotherly love, in honor giving preference to one another, not lagging in diligence, fervent in spirit, serving the Lord…continuing steadfastly in prayer." (Romans 12:10-12, NKJV)

Father in heaven, I thank You for the gift of Your Son Jesus Christ, through whom we have eternal life, forgiveness and peace. I pray Your will be done on earth, as it is in heaven.

I pray specifically that You surround me and my household with favor, so that the wealth of the wicked is turned over into our hands.

I pray for open doors and opportunities for ministry so that I can be an effective witness for You.

I confess that my church family is a church of excellence, comprised of people of excellence;

who are highly committed and richly blessed supernatural individuals.

We are anointed to produce outstanding and uncommon results in life. We walk by faith and not by sight and the love of God is perfected in us.

We are ever growing in numbers, and one hundred percent tithing members.

We receive everything necessary for the preaching of the Gospel, building, equipment, staff and finances.

I thank You for the opportunity to partake in this great commission; and share in the grace, anointing and the blessing of our pastor.

In Jesus' name! Amen!

Confessions for Tithes and Offerings

"Give and it will be given to you: good measure, pressed down, shaken together, and running over will be put into your bosom. For with the same measure that you use, it will be measured back to you." (Luke 6:38, NKJV)

Dear Heavenly Father, I thank You that You have brought me into an everlasting covenant of peace, blessing and prosperity; scaled by the blood of Your son, Jesus Christ.

You have redeemed me from darkness and translated me into Your marvelous light. And now I gladly worship You with my tithes and offerings.

I set my heart to seek first Your kingdom. In my cheerful giving, I demonstrate that You are my source and provider.

Your word assures me, that when I sow my seed in faith, I will also reap a harvest. So I speak now to my seed, to bring forth bountifully. I declare that this is my year of supernatural manifestation and I will eat the best of the land.

I command the north, the south, the east and the west, to release every good thing that belongs to me. I break all alliance with the spirit of poverty, lack and insufficiency and I enter into my wealthy place.

I thank You that I am blessed, living the abundant life. My household and my church family are blessed and together we are a blessing, until all the families of the earth are blessed. In Jesus' name, Amen!

Confessions for Your Children

"All your children shall be taught by the Lord, and great shall be the peace of your children." (Isaiah 54:13, NKJV)

Father in Heaven, I thank You this day for my children. I thank You that they are gifts from You. I thank You that my children belong to You and that You have entrusted me to care for them.

I thank You Father that I delight in You. According to Your covenant in Psalm 112 verse 2; my descendants will be mighty on earth. I thank You that the generation of the upright will be blessed. Therefore, I call my children blessed and mighty in their generation.

Dear God, I thank You that my children have a destiny. I pray that they will discover their destiny and purpose early in life. I thank You that they will not have to go through life wandering about. I thank You that they have the confidence of knowing who they are and their assignments in life.

I pray now for each of my children; that they will not spend years in futility. But they will be productively engaged at all times.

I declare over them the peace of God, the direction of God, the preservation of God and the will of God. I pray that none of my children will ever experiment with drugs, alcohol or sex. I declare that all my children will remain virgins until marriage. I declare that none of my children will ever experience divorce. I thank You that they have the wisdom of God to make right and wise choices in life. I thank You that my children have an understanding of what it means to seek the will of God.

None of what I went through will be their experience. I made certain mistakes in life, because I did not have the knowledge or the wisdom of God. But I thank You that my children now have what I did not have, a Godly heritage and Father. I thank You that they build upon that foundation to become all that You created them to be.

The Bible says in Proverbs 22:6 *"Train up a child in the way he should go, and when he is old he will not depart from it."* So Father, I thank You that the seed of the Word that I have sown in their hearts is alive. It will grow and produce an abundant harvest of righteousness, faithfulness, integrity and Godly character.

I thank You that my children are in the world, but they are not of the world. I thank You that they are shielded from the ferocious attacks of Satan. I thank You that no ungodly influence will uproot them from the training of the word. I thank You that no one will attack them to hurt them, physically, verbally or in any other way.

I declare that my children will never be taken advantage of by a predator or child molester. My children will never be victims of abuse. My children will never be initiated into a cult. No enchantment against my children will ever prevail. I build a hedge of protection over my children against witchcraft, and every satanic attack.

In the name of Jesus, I anoint my children and set them apart for God. I thank You Father for hearing my supplication over my children. I believe that I receive my petition; therefore it is so unto me and unto my children in Jesus' mighty name. Amen!

Dr. Emmanuel Favor

Prayer Lists

"The righteous cry, and the Lord heareth and delivered them out of all their trouble." (Psalms 34:17, NKJV)

Dr. Emmanuel Favor

Daily Confessions for Victorious Living

I pray for divine healing for the following individuals:

I pray for deliverance for the following individuals:

I pray that the following projects will be completed in record time:

_____

_____

_____

_____

_____

_____

_____

_____

_____

_____

_____

Dr. Emmanuel Favor

A Message From the Author

Words are a powerful force. They create our realities and determine the direction of our lives. The Bible teaches that we have whatever we say (Mark 11:20-23) and that death and life is in the power of the tongue (Proverbs 18:21).

It is especially important when we pray that we speak in accordance to the mind of God. James 5:16 tells us about the "effective, fervent prayer" of the righteous. If there can be an effective prayer, there can also be an ineffective prayer. Part of what makes prayer effective is when it is in accordance to the will or word of God.

Daily Confessions for Victorious Living, is written to help you construct your prayer life in accordance with what God says about you, so you can have what God has already planned for you. When you learn to say the same thing that God says, you will begin to see the manifestation of your confession.

This book is a must for anyone who wants a prayer life that produces results. It is a guide through prayers and confessions for life, family and others that you care about. Your prayer life will not remain the same if you apply these simple Bible based principles to prayer.

About The Author

Dr. Emmanuel Favor is a unique voice that speaks hope and grace to this generation. He is a pastor, teacher and motivational speaker, distinguished by his innovative spirit, forward thinking and an unquenchable passion for individual and community transformation.

He ministers the word with simplicity and understanding; his ministry has led him to speak to live audiences in more than a dozen countries and in four continents, both in the Christian as well as the secular arena. His integrity, humor and down-to-earth approach in delivering the Word, have earned him recognition, respect and the admiration of many.

Besides being a pastor, he is also an author and an entrepreneur who not only talks the talk, but also walks the walk when it comes to integrity, character and the exemplification of the principles of the Kingdom which he represents.

Pastor Favor holds a Bachelors of Theology degree from Trinity College of Ministerial Arts and an honorary doctorate in missions, awarded to him in recognition of his work and impact which cut across cultural and national boundaries.

He is the founder and Senior Pastor of Trailblazers International Christian Center, a thriving multi-cultural, non-denominational church in Baltimore, Maryland.

Daily Confessions for Victorious Living

Dr. Emmanuel Favor